INTEGRITY RISKS AND RED FLAGS IN
ENERGY PROJECTS

JANUARY 2023

ASIAN DEVELOPMENT BANK

Corrigenda to ADB publications may be found at http://www.adb.org/publications/corrigenda.

Notes:
References in this publication to bidders, bids, bid evaluation committees, and bid evaluation
reports are used within the context of the procurement of works (contractors), goods (suppliers),
and consulting and non-consulting services.

All photos by ADB except when otherwise stated.

In this publication, "$" refers to United States dollars.

On the cover: **Fiaga Power Plant in Samoa**. Components of the Fiaga Power Plant—a subproject
of the Power Sector Expansion Project managed by Electric Power Corporation—ensured the
improved capacity and efficiency of Samoa's power sector (photo by ADB).

Cover design by Paolo Tan.

CONTENTS

TABLES, FIGURE, BOXES, AND CHECKLISTS

TABLES

FIGURE

BOXES

CHECKLISTS

FOREWORD

Since 2003, the Asian Development Bank's Office of Anticorruption and Integrity has conducted proactive integrity reviews (PIRs) to identify and address control weaknesses that give rise to integrity risks in ongoing sovereign operations. Insights from these PIRs are published in this series, *Integrity Risks and Red Flags*.

This publication highlights weaknesses and red flags identified through PIRs of six energy projects financed by ADB. Further volumes in the series feature insights from five other sectors: agriculture, natural resources, and rural development; education; health; transport; and water. Through this sector-based series, governments, public bodies, and stakeholders engaged in designing and implementing projects can learn from past vulnerabilities and establish processes and controls to effectively mitigate integrity risks.

To help foster and sustain economic growth, ADB's Strategy 2030 underscores the strengthening of governance and institutional capacity as an operational priority in the bank's developing member countries. Let us achieve a prosperous, inclusive, resilient, and sustainable Asia and the Pacific by maintaining the highest ethical standards.

John Versantvoort
Head, Office of Anticorruption and Integrity
Asian Development Bank

ACKNOWLEDGMENTS

Integrity Risks and Red Flags in Energy Projects was prepared and developed collaboratively by H. Lorraine Wang (former advisor), Caridad Garrido Ortega (consultant and former senior integrity specialist), and Erickson M. Quijano (consultant) of the Preventive and Compliance Division, Office of Anticorruption and Integrity, Asian Development Bank.

This publication greatly benefited from the insights and comments of John Versantvoort (head), David Binns (former advisor), Lisa Kelaart-Courtney (director), Jung Min Han (senior integrity specialist), and Kristopher Marasigan (integrity officer) of the Office of Anticorruption and Integrity. This publication was made possible by the review from Yongping Zhai (former chief of Energy Sector Group, Sustainable Development and Climate Change Department).

ABBREVIATIONS

ADB	Asian Development Bank
BEC	bid evaluation committee
BER	bid evaluation report
OAI	Office of Anticorruption and Integrity
PIR	proactive integrity review

INTRODUCTION

Since the Asian Development Bank (ADB) adopted its Anticorruption Policy in 1998, fighting corruption has become embedded in ADB's broader work in governance, public administration, and capacity development.[1] The Anticorruption Policy affirms the bank's zero tolerance for corruption and lays the groundwork for supporting anticorruption efforts.

ADB's Strategy 2030 identifies strengthening governance and institutional capacity as one of seven operational priorities for a prosperous, inclusive, resilient, and sustainable Asia and the Pacific. The Office of Anticorruption and Integrity (OAI) promotes the implementation of this operational priority through a combination of activities aimed at (i) enforcement and (ii) prevention and compliance.

The proactive integrity review (PIR) is a mechanism used by ADB since 2003 to help prevent and detect integrity violations and address risks in ADB-financed or -administered projects. PIRs (i) identify and assess integrity risks in procurement, contract and asset management, and financial management of a project; and (ii) recommend measures to mitigate these risks and to ensure that project funds are used for their intended purposes.

PIRs evaluate the adherence of projects to three core principles of project integrity: (i) transparency—proper documentation of key decisions, public disclosure of project information, and protection of confidential information; (ii) fairness—objective and reliable bidding process and requirements optimizing competition, impartial evaluation, and a credible complaints mechanism; and (iii) accountability and control—accurate and timely project accounting and reporting, eligibility of expenditures and timely payments, adherence to contract provisions, and adequate project oversight and management.

OAI ensures that PIR knowledge is applied to the projects reviewed through follow-up reviews, at which time OAI verifies the implementation status of the PIR. In addition, OAI assists the executing and implementing agencies in addressing open recommendations.[2]

PIR knowledge is institutionalized in ADB operations through (i) embedding of PIR requirements in ADB guidance and instruction documents, (ii) integrity risk management reviews, (iii) knowledge enhancement and transfer workshops and other learning courses, and (iv) knowledge products.[3] Following a country-focused approach (one of three guiding principles outlined in Strategy 2030), PIR knowledge also informs the country partnership strategies of developing member countries.[4] Through this exercise, PIR knowledge is considered in designing new projects as the country partnership strategy predominantly drives country operations business plans.

This publication presents vulnerabilities from PIRs of six energy projects (Appendix) across five countries and three regions and highlights recommended measures to mitigate identified integrity risks.[5]

---

[1] ADB. 1998. *Anticorruption Policy*. Manila.

[2] The follow-up review reports document the implementation status of PIR recommendations (footnote 5).

[3] Through integrity risk management reviews, PIR knowledge is built in preapproval project documents (concept papers, reports and recommendations of the President to the Board of Directors, technical assistance reports).

[4] The country partnership strategy is the primary platform for defining ADB's operational focus in a developing member country.

[5] The energy projects reviewed were selected from all active ADB-financed loan and grant projects using a risk-based selection process. The selection process took into account the size of funding, lending modality, implementation arrangements, number of awarded contracts, level of disbursements, input from relevant ADB departments, prior project results, external benchmarking, and potential benefits of a proactive integrity review (PIR) to the project. PIR reports are available on the ADB website (*https://www.adb.org/who-we-are/integrity/proactive-integrity-review*).

SECTOR OVERVIEW

Energy demand is projected to almost double in Asia and the Pacific by 2030. Innovative ways to generate power in a socially, economically, and environmentally sustainable manner are urgently needed. Compounding the problem is widespread energy poverty across Asia and the Pacific, with 150 million people still without access to electricity in 2020.[6]

ADB has provided assistance to developing member countries in the energy sector for more than 40 years. The bank has been working to improve access to reliable, affordable, low-carbon energy across Asia and the Pacific through its various financing instruments and governance reform assistance.

Table 1 presents ADB's financial resources commitments in the energy sector from 2017 to 2021.

Table 1: ADB's Financing Commitments in the Energy Sector, 2017–2021

Year	2017	2018	2019	2020	2021
Value ($ million)	6,230	5,095	2,660	4,292	1,837
Percent of commitments in all sectors	28.59%	20.78%	11.08%	13.59%	8.07%

Source: Asian Development Bank. 2022. ADB Annual Report 2021. Manila.

---

[6] ADB's work in the energy sector: https://www.adb.org/what-we-do/sectors/energy/overview.

INTEGRITY RISKS AND RED FLAGS

Methodology

OAI identified and synthesized integrity-related vulnerabilities, including red flags, from all its energy PIR findings.[7] A vulnerability is any gap in a project's implementation processes that, if not remediated in a timely manner, will increase the likelihood of an integrity violation occurring and/or the impact of an integrity violation. In other words, the vulnerability increases the integrity risk profile of the project.

Integrity risk is the risk that project funds are diverted from their intended purposes due to fraud, corruption, or other integrity violations.[8] Integrity violations are more likely to occur if integrity risks are not detected or not addressed effectively and in a timely manner. Integrity risk management is an essential prerequisite for ensuring that projects achieve the intended development outcomes.

OAI assessed the level of vulnerabilities (high, medium, or low) by occurrence and impact.[9] This publication follows the project implementation processes and related subprocesses shown in Table 2. This document describes high- and medium-risk vulnerabilities and mitigating measures in each project implementation process.

Table 2: Project Implementation Processes

Process	Procurement	Contract and Asset Management	Financial Management
Subprocess	**A1 Bidding** Prequalification, bidding documents preparation, bid advertisements, submissions, and opening	**B1 Contract administration** The management of the day-to-day practicalities and administrative requirements under the contract	**C1 Expenditure management** Approval and processing of payments for project expenditures
	A2 Bid evaluation Assessment of bidders' compliance with bidding requirements, and preparation and approval of evaluation report	**B2 Output monitoring** Engagement with and/or supervision of contractors, consultants, and suppliers in relation to project outputs	**C2 Financial reporting** Project accounting and auditing
	A3 Contract award Post-bid evaluation activities until contract is awarded and signed	**B3 Asset control** Safeguarding and maintenance of project assets including asset inventory	

Note: The subprocesses reflect those prioritized by the Office of Anticorruption and Integrity and do not reflect all subprocesses that exist within each process.
Source: Office of Anticorruption and Integrity, Asian Development Bank.

---

[7] Red flags are indicators of irregularities, which may indicate the occurrence of integrity violations. Project staff should be alert to red flags indicative of integrity violations and promptly report potential violations to the OAI.

[8] Integrity violation is any act that violates ADB's Anticorruption Policy, including corrupt, fraudulent, coercive, or collusive practice, abuse, conflict of interest, obstructive practice, violations of ADB sanctions, retaliation against whistleblowers and witnesses, and failure to adhere to the highest ethical standards.

[9] OAI determined the occurrence of a vulnerability by establishing the frequency with which this was identified in the proactive integrity reviews; and based the impact of a vulnerability on the likelihood that this could have resulted in an integrity violation or misuse of project funds.

Integrity Risk Heat Maps

The heat map in Figure (a) shows the level of risk arising from the vulnerabilities identified in the energy PIRs and presented in the processes in which they manifested.[10] In the six energy projects reviewed, OAI identified high integrity risks in the procurement, and contract and asset management processes.

Figure (b) shows the risk level by subprocess. Risk levels are highest in bidding (A2) and financial reporting (C2) subprocesses.

Figure: Integrity Risk Heat Maps

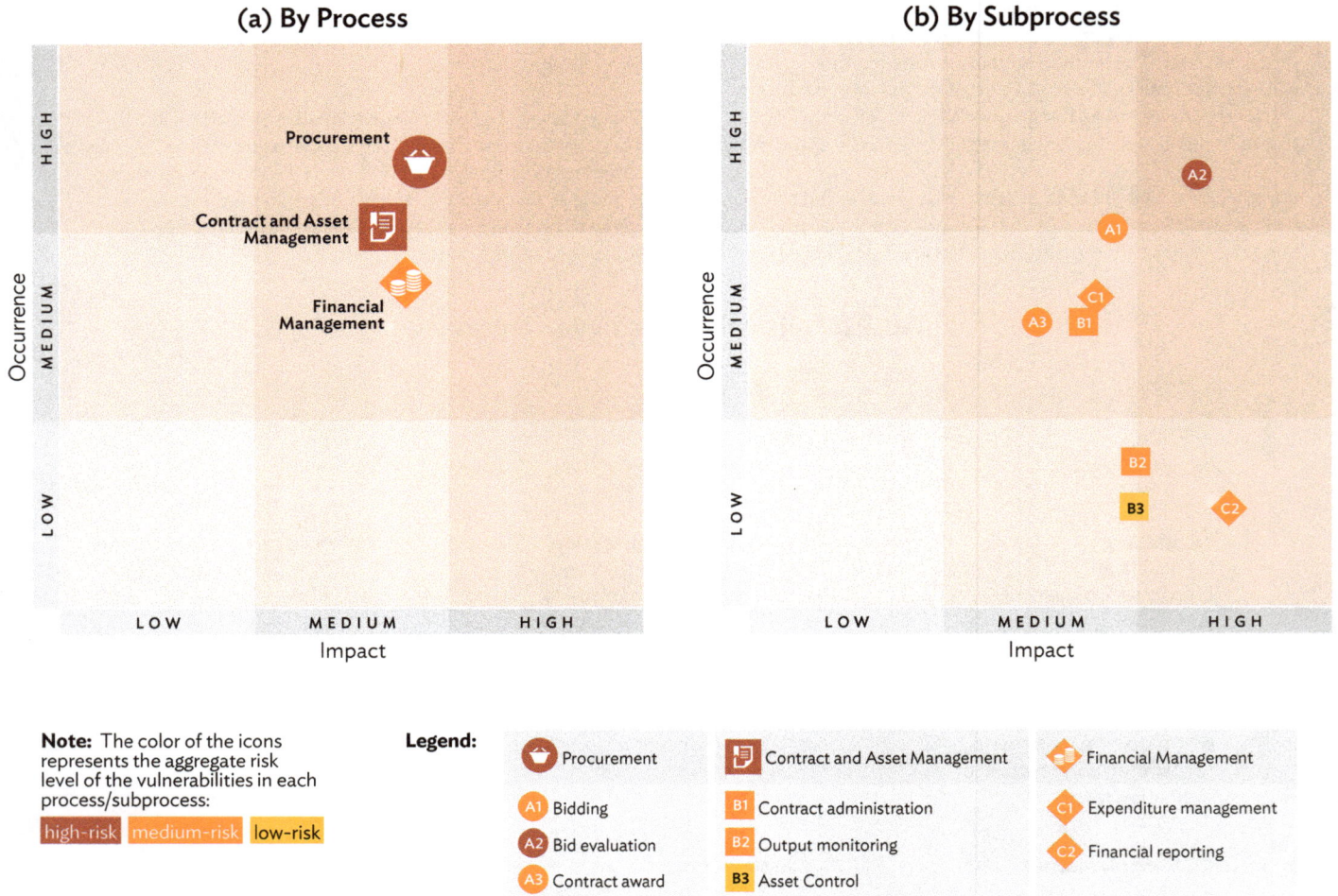

(a) By Process

(b) By Subprocess

Note: The color of the icons represents the aggregate risk level of the vulnerabilities in each process/subprocess:

high-risk   medium-risk   low-risk

Legend:

Procurement   Contract and Asset Management   Financial Management

A1 Bidding   B1 Contract administration   C1 Expenditure management

A2 Bid evaluation   B2 Output monitoring   C2 Financial reporting

A3 Contract award   B3 Asset Control

Source: Office of Anticorruption and Integrity, Asian Development Bank.

---

[10] The heat map is a visual representation of relationships among two sets of data: the likelihood that an integrity violation may occur (occurrence) and its potential impact to the project (impact).

Vulnerabilities and Mitigating Measures

OAI's analysis aimed to identify factors contributing to integrity vulnerabilities and to formulate risk mitigating measures. These measures may be applied to all projects regardless of their financing modality or structure. Project teams can use the due diligence checklists during bid evaluation (Checklist 1) and expenditure payment processing (Checklist 2) to identify and mitigate the risks.[11]

PROCUREMENT

(A1) Bidding

Red flags indicative of integrity violations. OAI identified red flags indicating that the fairness of the bidding process may have been undermined. These increase the likelihood of occurrence of fraud and corruption occurring that may jeopardize the project and alienate prospective bidders. Examples of red flags in bidding are summarized in Table 3.

Red flags are multifaceted, and those summarized in Table 3 may have one or a combination of the elements of collusion, fraud, corruption, and/or conflicts of interest.

Table 3: Examples of Red Flags in Bidding

Type of Integrity Violation	Red Flags
Collusive practice	**Ineligible bidders circumventing ADB's Anticorruption Policy** In a rebidding, the bid evaluation committee decided that three suppliers were substantially responsive to the bidding requirements. However, ADB had debarred two of these suppliers. The remaining supplier (i) appeared to be related to the two debarred suppliers, (ii) purchased bidding documents on the day of the bid submission deadline, and (iii) submitted a bid to create an illusion of competition.
	Leakage of confidential bidding information Negotiations between the project management unit and the supplier were initiated 2 months before quotations from other suppliers were sought.

ADB = Asian Development Bank.

Note: Collusive practice is an arrangement between two or more parties designed to achieve an improper purpose, including influencing improperly the actions of another party.

Source: Office of Anticorruption and Integrity, Asian Development Bank.

MITIGATING MEASURES
Red Flags Indicative of Integrity Violations

- ADB regional departments and resident missions should ensure that executing and implementing agencies, including project implementing units/offices and evaluation committees, understand their obligations under ADB's Anticorruption Policy, especially the obligation to report any integrity violation to OAI when such allegation is initially identified or suspected. Executing and implementing agencies should communicate these obligations to the bidders (contractors, consultants, suppliers), provide the necessary oversight, and conduct appropriate due diligence to minimize the risk of integrity violations on development projects.

- ADB regional departments and resident missions should ensure that all executing and implementing agencies handling procurement under ADB-financed projects have access to ADB's Complete Sanctions List (http://sanctions.adb.org).

---

[11] OAI rolled out project management checklists to help executing and implementing agencies self-assess (i) executing/implementing agency capacity, (ii) project procurement processes, (iii) financial management, and (iv) project output management from an integrity perspective. These checklists are available at https://www.adb.org/who-we-are/integrity/proactive-integrity-review.

PROCUREMENT

CONTRACT
AND ASSET
MANAGEMENT

FINANCIAL
MANAGEMENT

OTHER
VULNERABILITIES

(A2) Bid Evaluation

Vulnerabilities in bid evaluation can result in contracts awarded to unqualified bidders, thereby undermining the transparency and fairness of the procurement at an ultimate cost to the project. Process inconsistencies and deficiencies, and inaccurate evaluation results may create the impression of favoring bidders. If not addressed, these vulnerabilities may eventually lead to substandard outputs, delayed implementation, waste, loss of funds, or harm to the intended beneficiaries.

Inadequate due diligence. Bidders may provide dubious information on their eligibility, financial capacity, and experience. Without adequate due diligence during bid evaluation, bid evaluation committees (BECs) may fail to identify irregularities, inconsistencies, and/or potential misrepresentation.

Following a risk-based approach, the BEC should conduct due diligence to verify the submitted bid information against supporting documents (records check), from online sources (sanctions and other desktop research including previous adverse news), and/or from third parties (reference check). Combined with professional attributes such as a questioning mind and a critical assessment of documents, due diligence requires looking for indications of errors/misrepresentations on the documents, including checking the accuracy of information drawn from computations. The BEC should also seek clarifications/substantiation from bidders to the extent allowed by the bidding documents.

Examples of these evaluation errors resulting from the lack of or inadequate due diligence are summarized in Table 4. Box 1 presents sample cases of bid evaluation errors.

Table 4: Examples of Evaluation Errors

Bid Evaluation Aspect/Requirement	Nature of Evaluation Error
Financial capacity	• The evaluation accepted a bidder's outdated financial statements to support its financial capacity.
	• The evaluation used the value of a bidder's cash and cash equivalents declared in the bidding form, which was higher than the value in the submitted audited financial statements. ⚠
	• The bid evaluation committee (BEC) accepted the bidders' unaudited financial statements without first establishing that the law in the bidders' countries/jurisdictions did not mandate financial statements to be audited. By default, the bidding documents required submission of audited financial statements, while unaudited financial statements are allowed only on an exceptional basis.
	• The BEC overlooked the incorrect computation of net worth of a bidder.
	• The BEC accepted unsupported credit lines. ⚠
Eligibility	The BEC declared substantially responsive bids that were received from ADB-sanctioned bidders.
Personnel	The BEC incorrectly computed the years of experience based on the submitted curriculum vitae.
Pending litigation	The BEC inappropriately considered the bidder fully compliant with the requirements of the bidding documents even though the bidder did not disclose its pending litigation as indicated in the notes to the financial statements. ⚠

ADB = Asian Development Bank.

Legend: ⚠ = indicative of potential misrepresentation (fraudulent practice). Fraudulent practice is any act or omission, including a misrepresentation, that knowingly or recklessly misleads, or attempts to mislead, a party to obtain a financial or other benefit or to avoid an obligation.

Source: Office of Anticorruption and Integrity, Asian Development Bank.

Box 1: Cases—Bid Evaluation Errors

Case 1: Financial Capacity—Outdated Support
A bidder was found to have sufficient financial capacity and awarded a contract on the basis of outdated financial statements from 2-3 years earlier. The bid evaluation committee should have requested the most recent information on financial resources, including financial statements, and reassessed the bidder's financial capacity. At the time of the evaluation, the financial capacity requirements may not have been met by the bidder. In this case, the winning bidder's cash flows issues contributed to implementation delays.

Case 2: Financial Capacity—Questionable Financial Information
A bidder, a joint venture of firms A and B,

• declared firm A's cash and cash equivalents on the bidding form FIN-3: Availability of Financial Resources at a higher amount than what was reported in firm A's audited financial statements, and

• submitted, for firm B, annual earnings released in lieu of audited financial statements to support the financial information in its bid.

The bid evaluation committee overlooked both lapses and declared the bidders compliant with the financial capacity requirements.

TAKEAWAY
Rigorous review of the bidders' compliance with financial capacity requirements, particularly the review of the consistency of the financial resources declared on the bidding forms and audited financial statements, ensures that the winning bidders have sufficient financial resources to implement the contracts.

Source: Office of Anticorruption and Integrity, Asian Development Bank.

Inconsistent application of bid evaluation criteria. This may give the perception of favoring bidders or undue influence. Examples of inconsistent application of bid evaluation criteria are summarized in Table 5.

Table 5: Examples of Inconsistent Application of Bid Evaluation Criteria

Bid Evaluation Aspect/Requirement	Nature of Inconsistent Application of Bid Evaluation Criteria
Current contract commitments	One bidder submitted an incomplete form where current contract commitments were declared. The bid evaluation committee (BEC) treated this as a major deviation despite the advice of the evaluation consultant to seek clarifications from the bidder. In contrast, the BEC did not treat this as a major deviation for another bidder that submitted an incomplete current contract commitments form. ⚠
Proposed experts and subcontractors	The BEC requested clarifications and additional documents from some bidders for deficiencies in the proposed experts and subcontractor. However, the BEC disqualified some bidders for the same deficiencies without seeking clarifications from them. ⚠

Legend: ⚠ = indicative of potential bid manipulation (collusive practice). Collusive practice is an arrangement between two or more parties designed to achieve an improper purpose, including influencing improperly the actions of another party.
Source: Office of Anticorruption and Integrity, Asian Development Bank.

Absence of documentation to support bid evaluation decisions. The transparency of bid evaluation is diminished in the absence of documentation to substantiate the BEC's evaluation conclusions. Most of the PIR findings of this nature relate to consulting selections where shortlisting or evaluation decisions were unclear or unsupported by qualification criteria or a clearly defined rating system.

PROCUREMENT

CONTRACT
AND ASSET
MANAGEMENT

FINANCIAL
MANAGEMENT

OTHER
VULNERABILITIES

Inaccuracies in bid evaluation reports (BERs). Inadequate and unclear information in BERs may appear to conceal erroneous or subjective assessments favoring certain bidders. Examples of inaccurate information in BERs are summarized in Table 6.

Table 6: Examples of Inaccuracies in Bid Evaluation Reports

Bid Evaluation Report Item	Nature of Inaccurate and Incomplete Information in Bid Evaluation Reports
Joint venture arrangement	The bidders submitted their intent to form a joint venture after the bid submission deadline. This special case, including the bid evaluation committee's rationale for allowing it, was not discussed in the bid evaluation report (BER).
Completeness and substantial responsiveness to the bidding requirements	• The BER stated that a bid was complete in most respects and generally responsive to the bidding requirements. However, in another section of the same BER, the same bid was described as incomplete and substantially nonresponsive to the bidding requirements. • The BER indicated that only one bid was substantially responsive, yet the BER noted that two bidders' factories were visited as part of further evaluation. The proactive integrity review determined that one of the two bidders was not responsive to the financial requirements of the bidding documents, but this fact was not indicated in the BER.

Source: Office of Anticorruption and Integrity, Asian Development Bank.

MITIGATING MEASURES
Vulnerabilities in Bid Evaluation

• BEC members should undergo detailed and practical hands-on training on all aspects of bid evaluation, especially due diligence, before undertaking new bid evaluation assignments. Support from ADB regional departments, supervision consultants, and procurement experts is required (a checklist on how to avoid common errors/lapses in bid evaluation is on Checklist 1).

• ADB regional departments should perform rigorous reviews of BERs, particularly when the executing agency's procurement capacity is not robust or when contracts are high value, high risk, or complex. Rigorous review entails seeking

clarifications from the executing/implementing agencies, calling in bids on a sample basis, validating evaluation report information against bids, and assessing the reasonableness of significant evaluation committee decisions.

• The executing/implementing agency should hold pre-bid meetings for high-value, high-risk, or complex procurement, where bidding requirements are carefully discussed with bidders. The BEC must consistently apply these requirements.

• The executing/implementing agency should check accuracy and completeness of information in BERs before submitting these for ADB's no-objection. For transparency, decisions made and justifications for deviations should be reflected in the BERs.

Checklist 1: How to Avoid Common Errors and Lapses in Bid Evaluation

ADB Sanctions List

☐ Verify that the bidder (all parties to the joint venture/association/consortium agreement) is not on ADB's complete Sanctions List (https://sanctions.adb.org).

Construction Turnover

☐ Verify the turnover declared on the bidding form against the turnover reported in the audited financial statements submitted.

Financial Capacity

☐ Verify the financial capacity-related accounts (working capital, net worth) declared on the bidding form against the corresponding accounts in the audited financial statements submitted.

☐ Verify the credit lines declared against the supporting documents submitted.

Current Contract Commitments

☐ Verify the current contract commitments declared on the bidding form against the contract commitments reported in the audited financial statements submitted.

Experience

☐ Verify the experience declared on the bidding form against the work completion certificates (for works) and curricula vitae (for experts/consultants) submitted.

Pending Litigation

☐ Verify the pending litigations declared on the bidding form against the pending litigation disclosures in the audited financial statements submitted.

Criteria Requiring Computations

☐ Recompute the amounts on the bidding forms and verify that any formulas used, including the exchange rates, are correct.

ADB = Asian Development Bank, OAI = Office of Anticorruption and Integrity.
Note: Where a red flag is identified, refer it to OAI for further verification.
Source: Office of Anticorruption and Integrity, Asian Development Bank.

(A3) Contract Award

Inappropriate contract negotiations after contract award and prior to signing. Negotiations after contract award seriously impair the transparency of the procurement process. They give contractors legal grounds to argue misprocurement, which could result in lengthy legal proceedings and implementation delays.

Under open competitive bidding, the employer (executing agency) must invite bids based on well-defined qualification requirements and technical specifications. Bidders provide unconditional offers, and the employer may accept (without conditions) the lowest responsive bid.

In a civil works contract, the executing agency and the lowest evaluated substantially responsive bidder held extensive negotiations on technical specifications following the issuance of acceptance letter (notification of award) and prior to contract signing. Agreement between the executing agency and the contractor on the technical specifications was presented as a condition for contract signing. The procurement process did not permit contract award conditions to be imposed on contractors that complied with bidding requirements.

MITIGATING MEASURES
Contract Negotiations after Contract Award and Prior to Signing

Deviations, reservations, and omissions in bids should be addressed by strictly following the bid evaluation process as outlined in the instructions to bidders, instead of through contract negotiations. Disposition of deviations and other issues in bids should be documented in the BER.

CONTRACT AND ASSET MANAGEMENT

B1 Contract Administration

Inadequate vetting of a proposed additional subcontractor. Not appropriately assessing the qualifications of proposed substitute and/or additional subcontractors post-contract award increases the risk of the subcontractor not meeting the qualifications required to implement the contract. This may lead to further additions, substitutions, and cost overruns.

In a civil works contract, the executing agency did not thoroughly review a contractor's request to add a subcontractor (i.e., subcontractor not nominated in the bid) prior to approving the same. The proposed subcontractor (i) was not an established construction company; (ii) was not an experienced civil works firm; and (iii) had been dissolved, i.e., had no legal personality at the time it was engaged by the contractor, rendering it incapable of entering into contracts. This circumvented the bid evaluation process since evaluation of the winning bidder's capacity did not consider the complete roster of subcontractors that would be engaged to complete the works.

> **MITIGATING MEASURES**
> ### Inadequate Vetting of a Proposed Additional Subcontractor
>
> The executing agency should obtain documentation from the contractor establishing the proposed subcontractor's compliance with the requirements of the contract, including eligibility. The executing agency should be satisfied with the contractor's vetting procedures (as verified by the supervision consultant) and its results.

B2 Output Monitoring

Use of substandard materials and works that were substandard, defective, or off-specifications. Executing and implementing agencies should ensure that contractors, consultants, and suppliers are adequately supervised and that any issues are addressed in a timely manner. The PIR asset inspection of energy projects identified output defects, deviations from approved designs/specifications, and use of substandard materials, which could have been detected and rectified earlier had the project supervision been more robust. This inadequate supervision of contractors by supervision consultants and executing/implementing agencies resulted in delays, acceptance of works that were substandard, and cost overruns. Box 2 shows an example of this issue.

> ### Box 2: Example—Use of Substandard Materials and Works that were Substandard, Defective, or Off Specifications
>
> In a power transmission project, quality and workmanship issues were observed during the proactive integrity review inspection in three subprojects across four project sites. Though these should not affect the overall performance of the plants and auxiliary structures, the sheer number of defects signifies poor quality controls by the contractor and supervision consultants. These may ultimately decrease the longevity of the constructed facilities.
>
> Source: Office of Anticorruption and Integrity, Asian Development Bank.

MITIGATING MEASURES
Use of Substandard
Materials and Substandard/
Defective Works

- Erring contractors, consultants, and suppliers should be held accountable to ensure that they fulfill their contractual obligations. This entails enforcing relevant penalty clauses and reporting poor performance to ADB without delay.

- For decentralized, complex, or high-risk projects, independent third-party monitoring firms should be engaged to augment the monitoring

activities performed by executing/implementing agencies, ADB regional departments, and supervision consultants.

- Executing/implementing agencies should closely monitor the supervision consultants. This entails rigorous review of the consultants' progress reports and, as necessary, verification of progress through field visits. A guide that provides a practical framework for field visits/ asset inspections can be accessed through this link: https://www.adb.org/sites/default/files/institutional-document/431571/asset-inspection-project-integrity.pdf.

FINANCIAL MANAGEMENT

C1 Expenditure Management

Ineligible expenditures. Executing and implementing agencies should counter the risk of payments made for ineligible expenditures. Expenditures that are (i) not within the contract terms, (ii) inadequately or inappropriately supported, or (iii) unauthorized are considered ineligible. These indicate that claims were not thoroughly reviewed against contract provisions. They provide opportunities for fraud and expose the project to the risk of loss of funds. Table 7 presents examples of ineligible expenditures.

Table 7: Examples of Ineligible Expenditures

Expenditure Category	Lapse/Gap in the Expenditure
Contractors' progress billings	• The executing agency paid the advance in full despite the contractor not complying with the condition for release of the advance, i.e., 75% advance would be paid upon delivery of the materials at the construction site. The contractor had not yet made any deliveries when it received the advance.
	• In at least 16 instances across 7 contracts, the executing agency continued making payments after contracts expired by 1 day to about 2 years. Expired contracts exposed the project to the risk of contractors not performing or poorly performing without recourse.
	• The executing agency approved claims without verifying completion of works for which the claims were being made. Required completion certificates issued by a third party were not attached to the claims.
Goods	The executing agency approved payments based on proforma invoices without any supporting documents that indicated completion of delivery, inspection, acceptance, and installation (as appropriate) of goods.

Source: Office of Anticorruption and Integrity, Asian Development Bank.

PROCUREMENT

CONTRACT
AND ASSET
MANAGEMENT

**FINANCIAL
MANAGEMENT**

OTHER
VULNERABILITIES

MITIGATING MEASURES
Ineligible Expenditures

- Before endorsing claims for payment, executing and implementing agencies should ensure that (i) payment approval procedures are followed, (ii) supporting documents are checked for accuracy and completeness, and (iii) details in the claims are validated against the contracts and supporting documents. Payments should be refused or reduced in line with relevant contractual provisions for works or services that were not performed or goods that were not delivered. (A checklist on how to avoid common errors/lapses in expenditure payment processing is on Checklist 2.)

- ADB regional departments and resident missions should ensure that executing and implementing agencies, including project implementing units/offices, understand their obligations under ADB's Anticorruption Policy, especially the obligation to report any integrity violations to OAI without delay when they are initially identified or suspected.

Checklist 2: How to Avoid Common Errors and Lapses in Expenditure Payment Processing

All Types

☐ Verify the claim against the milestone payment terms stipulated in the contract (including contract variations).

☐ Check whether the payment information indicated in the claim matches with the payment information in the contract.

☐ Identify any red flags on the supporting documents submitted, e.g., erasures, alterations, or other errors, and ask for clarifications.

Works (Contractors)

☐ Verify the claim against interim payment certificates/certificates of completion. Check if there are claims on nonwork days (work on a weekend or holiday with no preapproval).

Services (Consultants)

☐ Verify the remuneration claim (for input-based contracts) against detailed timesheets submitted.

☐ Verify claims for reimbursable expenses against supporting documents as required in the contract (not applicable for full lump-sum contracts), including:
  ○ Travel costs—proof of travel (tickets, receipts, boarding passes);
  ○ Accommodation—proof of stay (hotel bills, invoices, receipts); and
  ○ Seminars and workshops—attendance sheets, invoices or receipts for workshop costs like venue and equipment rental and refreshments.

Goods (Suppliers)

☐ Verify the claim against sales invoice and delivery receipt/proof that goods have been delivered, inspected, accepted, and, as necessary, properly installed.

Note: Where a red flag is identified, refer it to OAI for further verification.
Source: Office of Anticorruption and Integrity, Asian Development Bank.

◇ C2 Financial Reporting

Inadequate and unreliable accounting systems. To ensure that financial information is provided in a timely and accurate manner for project implementation and progress monitoring purposes, executing/implementing agencies should maintain adequate and reliable project accounting systems and apply accounting standards acceptable to ADB. Inadequate and unreliable systems increase (i) the risk of undetected integrity violations, noncompliance, and other irregularities; and (ii) the risk of making an unsound project management decision based on faulty financial information. Common PIR findings for this vulnerability include the non-maintenance of separate project accounts and discrepancies between the project and ADB financial records.

MITIGATING MEASURES
Inadequate and Unreliable
Accounting Systems

- Project accounts should be maintained separately from other projects and activities of executing/implementing agencies.

- Periodic account reconciliations between (i) project accounts and ADB financial records; and (ii) project accounts and bank records should be performed monthly or quarterly, as necessary and practicable, and any discrepancies should be immediately addressed.

OTHER INTEGRITY-RELATED VULNERABILITIES THAT CUT ACROSS PROJECT IMPLEMENTATION PROCESSES

Integrity risks in project implementation principally result from the executing/implementing agency's capacity gaps—particularly in procurement, contract and asset management, financial management processes, and in maintaining project records.

D1 Executing and Implementing Agency's Capacity

Inadequate technical capacity on ADB operational guidelines and procedures. Project staff of executing and implementing agencies should be knowledgeable on ADB procurement, financial management, and disbursement guidelines and procedures. Given the observed frequent staff turnover and high dependence on consultants, executing and implementing agencies should ensure that this institutional knowledge is retained, transferred, and refreshed.

MITIGATING MEASURES
Staff Capacity Issues

To ensure that institutional knowledge and practices over ADB operational guidelines and procedures are retained, transferred, and refreshed, executing and implementing agencies

with assistance from ADB as necessary should develop an onboarding kit for new staff that includes primers and manuals. Regular relevant trainings should be undertaken for all staff and a quality assurance or monitoring process should be implemented under the guidance of, or with assistance from ADB, as required.

D2 Records Management

Missing or disorganized key project documents and absence of suitable records management. Inaccurate or incomplete audit trail of project activities complicates the timely prevention and detection of integrity violations, noncompliance, and errors. Executing and implementing agencies should maintain an effective records management system that evidences their compliance with anticorruption, procurement, financial management, and other relevant guidelines.

MITIGATING MEASURES
Records Management Issues

Executing and implementing agencies should establish and maintain an effective system of

records management to (i) facilitate records identification, validation, storage, and retrieval; (ii) improve accountability; (iii) drive timely detection of errors and irregularities; and (iv) prevent misplacement.

CONCLUSION

Through its proactive integrity reviews of six energy projects, ADB's Office of Anticorruption and Integrity identified vulnerabilities and red flags in (i) procurement, (ii) contract and asset management, and (iii) financial management processes. Key vulnerabilities are summarized in Table 8.

To manage related risks, ADB encourages project staff to apply the mitigating measures recommended in this publication and use the due diligence checklists for bid evaluation (Checklist 1) and expenditure payment processing (Checklist 2). Project staff must remain alert to red flags of integrity violations and report suspected violations to the Office of Anticorruption and Integrity.

Integrity risks are generally elevated in complex, decentralized projects (i.e., large-scale projects involving numerous project components, geographical locations, and implementing entities). These projects benefit from strong accountability and control mechanisms that clarify responsibilities at each implementation level (from the executing agency down to the last implementing unit), and from closer supervision by the executing agency and ADB. Integrity-related controls should be embedded in contracts, manuals, and other authoritative documents.

Under Operational Priority 7 of Strategy 2030, ADB has committed to support governments in their efforts to eradicate corruption and to implement anticorruption measures in all its projects and programs. We trust that the insights compiled in this publication will contribute to these endeavors.

Table 8: High- and Medium-Risk Vulnerabilities in Energy Projects and their Implications

Process	Subprocess	Vulnerability	Risk Implication
Procurement	**A1** Bidding	Collusion among bidders and executing agencies	Conflicts of interest, fraud, and corruption jeopardizing the project and alienating prospective bidders
	A2 Bid evaluation	Inadequate due diligence, inconsistent application of bid evaluation criteria, absence of documentation to support bid evaluation decisions, and inaccuracies in bid evaluation reports	Diminished transparency and fairness of the bid evaluation subprocess resulting in contract awards to unqualified bidders
	A3 Contract award	Contract negotiations after contract award and prior to signing	Diminished transparency of the contract award subprocess that may result in bidders seeking declaration of misprocurement, which may potentially lead to implementation delays
Contract and asset management	**B1** Contract administration	Inadequate vetting of a proposed subcontractor	Hiring of unqualified subcontractor resulting in further substitutions and cost overruns
	B2 Output monitoring	Use of substandard materials and acceptance of works that were substandard, defective, or off specifications resulting from the inadequate monitoring of contractors by executing/implementing agencies and supervision consultants	Implementation delays, inferior quality of outputs, and cost overruns
Financial management	**C1** Expenditure management	Ineligible, unsupported, or inaccurate expenditures that were paid resulting from weaknesses in the review and analysis of claims	Heightened opportunities for fraud resulting in potential loss of project funds; potential threat to subsequent maintenance or warranty claims
	C2 Financial reporting	Inadequate and unreliable accounting systems	Greater risk of not detecting integrity violations, noncompliance, and other irregularities

Flawed project management decisions based on inaccurate financial information |

Source: Office of Anticorruption and Integrity, Asian Development Bank.

APPENDIX
List of Proactive Integrity Reviews of Energy Projects

Country	Project	PIR Report Issuance Date
Bhutan	Second Green Power Development Project	Nov 2019
Nepal	Rural Electrification, Distribution, and Transmission Project	Mar 2007
Pakistan	Power Transmission Enhancement Investment Program – Tranches 1 and 2	Oct 2014 Dec 2015 *(follow-up)*
Samoa	Power Sector Expansion Project	Jun 2012 Jun 2015 *(follow-up)*
Uzbekistan	Talimarjan Power Project	May 2016

PIR = proactive integrity review.

Note: Publication of full proactive integrity review reports started in 2008. Proactive integrity review reports prior to 2008 published on the Asian Development Bank website only contain report abstracts/summaries. The Pakistan Power Transmission Enhancement Investment Program has been counted as two separate projects: Tranche 1 (Sovereign Project 37192-023) and Tranche 2 - (Sovereign Project 37192-033).

Source: Office of Anticorruption and Integrity, Asian Development Bank.

www.ingramcontent.com/pod-product-compliance
Lightning Source LLC
Chambersburg PA
CBHW050059220326
41599CB00045B/7469